Energy Architecture and Engineering: Human Energy Systems of Tomorrow

Foundations of Engineering

By S.B. Robinson

Human Energy Systems of Tomorrow, Energy Architecture
and Engineering: Human Energy Systems of Tomorrow

Copyright 2022 S.B. Robinson

ISBN: 978-0-578-37657-8

Bound Paperback Edition printed February, 2022
Corrigendum Update printed August, 2022

Disclaimer: This manual will teach you the foundations of Energy
Engineering, providing you the necessary process to experience
fractal consciousness and create your reality in the native language
of the universe: energy.

This work is dedicated to countless lives who have come before us, whose actions stand testament to the reality in which we are blessed to participate. It is truly the greatest gift we each get to contribute to the world. Our actions will touch the end of time.

I wish to express my deepest gratitude to my family. You all are equally a part of me, and it is my loving honor to carry this contradiction in all that I do. I could not have accomplished this work without the care, patience, love, and understanding you have given me throughout the many stages of my life.

To my mentors, it has been your steadfast wisdom and sometimes fierce compassion that pushed me where I needed challenges and held me back where I needed to be polished. You are a force of nature, and my gratitude for your lessons is eternal.

Table of Contents

Author's Introduction 9

Prerequisites for Engineering..11

Introducing Human Energy Systems: Linear Consciousness 13

Handy References 22

Lesson 1: Learning How to Listen to Energy 23

Lesson 2: Understanding the Language of Energy...............39

Lesson 3: Conversations in Energy.....................................51

Lesson 4: Asking Questions and Understanding Answers.................61

Lesson 5: Thinking in Energy 70

Lesson 6: Testing in Reality 78

Lesson 7: Connecting with Gravity....................................90

Lesson 8: Preparing for Energy Architecture 95

Final Thoughts...101

If you are seeking an expansive understanding of your consciousness and the energy systems we use to communicate across the myriad of dimensions in the 21st Century, this manual is for you. Together, we will explore the building blocks of consciousness and how to create experiences with energy beyond 'normal' **Linear Consciousness** that, for the moment, defines many of your limitations. You will learn how to free your awareness from external restraints. To re-create the realities you live in using the tools and energy systems freely available to us today.

What do I mean by Linear Consciousness?

Linear consciousness is what each of us learned at the beginning of standardized education. It is how we arrange our experiences based on sensation and reaction: we experience external forces 'beyond our control' and react to this experience based on our memories of previous experiences.

For example: as a child, I'm sure most of us have had the experience of some sort of year-end testing. We sit in lectures and read books, we take a test, we are graded on what we remember, and end up with a very binary "pass or fail". This binary result often informed us of how we would be expected to feel, and probable experiences in our future.

In this configuration of consciousness, a person waits for an external event to inform the level of awareness to become. Another way to describe this style of consciousness is that Linear is the use of stories to change our energy.

There must first be an experience in linear consciousness, then a reaction that allows me to become a 'new' version of myself. The words I speak become the level of consciousness others will meet me at. "I" become the product of my reaction to the energy of my experiences. This experience in linear time determines my state of consciousness.

In Energy Architecture and Engineering, what I am offering you is the opportunity to learn another way of arranging your consciousness, one that is purely authentic to YOU, at a level deeper than energy, and in harmony with Reality, Truth, and Natural Law. I call this arrangement "Fractal Consciousness".

What is Fractal Consciousness?

Fractal consciousness is the infinitely complex and constantly generating patterns of awareness that repeat across different octaves of consciousness in increasing complexity. Quite the mouthful, I know. Bear with me!

By repeating a process of dividing aspects of this consciousness and experiencing the patterns in the many dimensions of human energy systems, our awareness grows in complexity beyond the limitations of 'memory' and 'energy.'

The purpose of an Architect or Engineer maintaining their presence in Fractal Consciousness means holding multiple layers of awareness together consciously. In short, your state of consciousness is unrestricted by the energy of others' words and actions.

There is a space between the linear and the fractal layers of awareness. This space-between can be viewed as the physical manifestation of 'zero'. It encompasses all things within all possibilities without limitation, and because of this, it can only be considered when filtered or limited. The filters manifest what the viewer expects to perceive. However, the mind is a self-writing program. We choose what filters stay in place. We can clean these lenses of reality to sharpen and adjust the light of the multiverse in the hologram of mind, to learn how to create something beautiful.

In linear consciousness, we are immersed in a reality that demands the pursuit of pre-packaged and easily repeatable experiences. The repeatability of these experiences becomes the justification for their continued existence, and the individual capacity for reason is kept inundated with tsunamis of potentially irrelevant data to sort through. The individual's heart is governed through cultural virtues of failed civilizations thousands of years out of context to the environments they were once required. Our linear experience of

7

reality has been built by countless multitudes of individual lives over the centuries who reacted in fear to their bodies and their experience of reality, which brings us to the world as it exists today. These fears and limitations may have serves us, once. But now is the time to begin to ask yourself if they still serve a purpose in your life.

My goal for this book is to teach you a different way to work with energy in a new way. Learning how to step out of Linear Consciousness and into the Fractal will change the way you know yourself and how you hold the balances of your inner universe. It will not simplify your life like some magic spell or pharmaceutical pill, but it will bring you a greater understanding of the multidimensional reality from which you were born.

Keep in mind that simply reading this book will not make you an Energy Engineer or Architect. This accomplishment requires the direct experiences of Fractal Consciousness, which this manual will guide you to put into action. The primary method to becoming an Energy Engineer is to achieve conscious and deliberate control of the energy that creates your experiences. You will be able to make a change in your consciousness, from Linear to Fractal.

Author's Introduction

I like to think that every generation who has ever lived on this planet has had an 'aha' moment, one that forever changed their civilization. That moment when they discovered something entirely new by using a pearl of pioneering wisdom, technology, or a wild understanding of the way things could be tomorrow. When I take a step back from this idea, I catch a glimpse of things they might have feared; maybe they feared not being enough to handle the challenges of their age. Perhaps the generations to go before them were wrong and handed them a bad deal, or all of their suffering and struggling would be for nothing. In the end, it would always seem to boil down to one radical notion that forces their cultures and civilizations to expand and grow in ripples that reshape what humanity is capable of. New Systems of thinking allowed ideas like Newton's *Second Law*, Darwin's *Theory of Evolution*, and Kekule's dream of the benzene molecule to form like rainbows in the mind.

It might be time, now, for a new idea to make its ripple in the pond of human consciousness.

That said, please let me introduce myself.

I have been exploring and teaching fractal consciousness explicitly for over a decade.

I started my career as an enlisted Marine who specialized in Tactical Data Network Engineering in my youth. I've worked under multiple Fortune 500 companies in these last ten years, including Microsoft, Amazon, and Nike. For eight wonderful years, I have served on the Board of Directors for an amazing non-profit organization, 'Interfaith Enlightenment Center'. I have also received several certifications for Neurolinguistic Programming and Neuro-hypnotic Repatterning under Dr. Richard Bandler, raised a son, and generally lived life at extremes of experience.

I've done so much more than 'worked' at those placed, however. I watched organizations rise and fall; I've watched the moon send a circle of desert wanderers into ecstatic bliss, and I've seen the energy grids of the planet expose a hidden heartbeat beneath Sufi Shrines in India. I've studied Tantric Vajrayana Buddhism at the Sakya Monastery of Tibetan Buddhism and received numerous empowerments to bridge consciousness to other dimensions for the benefit of all sentient beings. I've confronted and subdued, and worked with displaced Djinn affected by the unit rotations in Iraq. I've meditated at Stonehenge and Avebury and received the Initiations of The Quarry.

Through all these experiences and so many more, I've learned deeper truths about what energy is, what it means to work with it, and how the future of human energy systems can grow from this understanding.

It is truly my honor to share this understanding with you.

Prerequisites for Engineering

The Goal of Engineering is to give you the tools and experience necessary to be proficient in creating your experience of reality at an energetic level. While there is no way to enforce these prerequisites to Energy Architecture and Engineering, there are several factors you will need to understand to be successful.

The first factor to success in Energy Engineering is to have a clearly defined support team. These are the people, stories, symbols, or things that will be available when you need them to remind you of the best version of who you are and where you want to be in your life. Identify them now and keep them close. Wait to go forward if you're missing a support structure in your life: the Fractal can wait. Your wellbeing takes priority here.

The second factor is a moral principle: have respect. Respect yourself and the experiences that have brought you to this moment. These experiences are the most valuable resource you'll ever acquire. Respect the experiences that people around you have; they are moving from their own needs and missions. They cannot have your experience any more than you can have theirs.

A third factor is a necessary form of wisdom: knowing the difference between a want and a need. In Fractal Consciousness, a want is based on indirect knowledge: it represents the need for someone else's reality you choose to adopt as your own in many cases. Do you understand what that want means? Do you agree to the experience of being changed by that desire and the changes it will make in your consciousness for having it? Pay attention to where it may have overwritten your personal need: the experiences you are calling in explore the expansive consciousness that you are.

The fourth factor is the ability to recognize causal relationships in the symbols that show up in your dreams and daydreams. In simplest terms, downward causation can be an environmental trigger to an internal change, whereas upward causation is an internal trigger to an external change. Something to keep in the back of your mind as you progress in this training.

I also want to spend some time explaining our 'homework' given at the end of each lesson: Integration Projects. These projects are necessary for the direct experience and integration of Energy Architecture and Engineering. They are designed to build dictionaries and maps for your inner universe. These symbols are yours alone, the map to how energy has attached to memory, and how your unconscious mind translates this energy using the sense of thought. Without these keys of direct experience, the following lessons and their texts will remain as mental curiosities only, with no gravity behind them for you to take the necessary movements to achieve a fractal state of consciousness.

Take as long as you need between lessons to integrate them, but do not skip them.

Introducing Human Energy Systems: Linear Consciousness

Let us begin our exploration of Linear Consciousness by giving credit where credit is due. Human energy systems have come a long way in the last 5200+ years since civilization and language bloomed across this planet. We started with the barest minimum; the energy of breath, water, light, and food flowing in neat meridians through the physical body, flows that could create mighty feats of martial arts or incredibly restoring harmony between the body's organs. The Chinese called it chi, also referred to as prana in Hindu philosophy. It is the basis for many energy practices today, from acupuncture and martial arts like tai chi and qigong to yoga and kundalini awakening practices.

However, what gets very little attention is what happens after we use that primordial energy. We need to begin to pay attention to how this energy is attached to memory and how memory manifests that energy each time it is remembered. The act of remembering causes energy to flow through your energy field from a space beyond your chakras and auric field. Ask any Reiki healer how your mood affects your energy and vice versa. Your aura is a giant lens, focused on the world around you and filtering what you pay attention to.
Simply put, energy attaches to memory.

Remembered energy creates your energetic lens of perception. So, if you want to grow your perception or expand what you are capable of doing, this is where it begins. The key is in your memory.

You see, the mind is as much an organ like the heart. One of its functions is to perceive this energy and tell a story about what it sees changing. The subconscious is a fantastic ally in this function, attaching symbols to energy and telling a story of what it perceives as changes in your awareness. Have you ever had a dream that made perfect sense while asleep, only to find that explaining it on waking was almost impossible? That is the language of energy that your subconscious speaks, which does not translate easily to the logic of structured languages spoken between people.

Let's look at why this creates such a sense of disconnect and struggle.

Your mind is fantastic at sensing energy. It can coordinate between all of your physical senses and analyze the information against a lifetime of memory <u>instantly</u>. Don't believe me? Think of an apple, a specific one. Describe it. I'll wait.

Make some notes here. Describe the details that come to mind:

So, how did your apple look? What color was it? Can you recall just how many 'apples' you thought of before you decided on an answer?

Try it again. Think of a red apple.

How many memories did you experience when you thought of a red apple?

Is it a real apple you ate, or a plastic toy from your childhood?

Was one of those memories of a magnet, or maybe even a picture from a classroom wall?

Did you see any of these in your mind's eye as the questions were asked?

Did you skip any of these questions? What are you avoiding?

You might begin to notice some energies from memory are grouped by how you feel about them. More than any logical organization, personal preference plays a huge role in the memories you choose to create your reality (e.g., 'green apple' or 'plastic toy').

That's the trick. One might even call it a trap.

Sometimes we get attached to how we think a symbol looks to other people. We want that story our minds tell us to repeat the same every time, taking comfort from the familiar, without considering how our subconscious sees the energy changing. This simple disconnect is the root of our struggle in this day in age.

We want our memory to behave like textbook knowledge, to be a scientifically repeatable definition of what can be experienced repeatedly. We develop complex communication rituals and receive great comfort from these predictable habits. The collection of these energies from patterns, over time, becomes the basis of a culture, a dependable structure to the way these rituals can predictably exchange energy between people.

Let's review what some cultures suggest to us about what we can experience:

Looking for a spiritual experience? Look to the culture of entheogens or places of worship.

Looking for a rich experience? Look to the culture of economics, investment, and the stock market.

Looking for a dramatic experience? Look to the culture of cinema, drama, and Hollywood.

And yet, these experiences are always circular. Spiritual experiences come with highs and lows, wealth comes and goes, and no amount of drama will ever be satisfying. These cultures are fantastic at sharing needs, less about fulfilling them in a lasting, meaningful way. This structure of energy from culture is a double-edged sword. One side gives structured, energetic growth to individuals, but the other side limits those same individuals; they can only grow as much as the energy within this structure. Once you've contained the energy from one culture, that's it. You've hit the limit of growth possible and must now decide: do you attempt to grow and change the culture you are in to meet your need? Or do you seek out a different culture that gives you the necessary energy to become more than what you are now?

Before we go any further, let's review the facts we have explored so far.

Energy attaches to memory.

The body continuously cycles energy by collecting it from digested foods, sunlight, breath, and interacting with other living beings. This energy is spent during physical movement or strong emotion that produces a physical reaction (whether or not you acted on it).

When others observe one person's reactions, the energy they project along with a subconscious symbol is stored in the observer's memory. Each observer might store the energy in different octaves, depending on their focus of awareness. As that memory is triggered, whether intentionally or not, the initial band of energy is transmitted out from the physical body, often referred to as the aura.

This continuous cycle of energy and memory is how the energy structure of cultures and subcultures are defined, maintained, and transmitted between individuals.

Energetic Phases group memories.

Do you recall earlier when you were asked about your specific apple? If you allowed the experience to happen, it would have shown you that actively remembered energies would be entirely 'manifest' in your aura as the lens of your perception. The memory of eating an apple would be present in your aura. Still, all the examples that you could not remember until after being prompted represent 'unmanifest' energy that you contain but are not actively using. Manifest Energy is the memory that defines the scope of your awareness and limits your possible reactions.

In the same way that the mind collects symbols in phases, cultures gather potential experiences from people.

Phases are energetically isolated.

Phases are expressed as organically generated fractal structures of consciousness. Bear with me here; I know that's a big one. One phase will flow into the next phase by using symbols containing energy from the previous one that simultaneously bridges many phases. Let's look at how these manifests in daily life: identifying a need to buy groceries.

Let's consider your pantry as an aspect of consciousness. It is a dimension of space for the need of 'hunger' to exist. Your pantry is low, so you identify a need for more groceries and make a decision to start getting these groceries now. You write down a list of symbols based on how they previously made you feel. You take your list with you in your vehicle to purchase the items.
You enter the store, identify, select your appropriate items, pay for them, and return home. You array the new things in your pantry based on habit, memory, or convenience and decide the need to obtain groceries has been met. Grocery stores are rarely 'consciousness expanding' locations, are they? To understand why, we need the next fundamental principle.

No Structure can grow beyond the energies that support it.

Energy is the root of direct experience; it is a tension between the polarities of a divided aspect of awareness. The dividing force is described as a need of consciousness. The needs we have attached to specific symbols determines the level of consciousness that symbol represents in our awareness. We will go in depth about the 'hows' and 'whys' of this in the Lessons that follow.

All of this leads us to the fifth principle, the one that has kept us confined in a cycle of repeating the same experiences.

Feeling energy changes nothing. Containing energy changes everything.

The sensation of feeling energy is the mind observing a shift in tension between divided aspects of awareness. The function of the mind, as a sensory organ, includes the sensing of energy. It describes observations using symbols that are energy attached in memory.

19

Like having a daydream, moving the symbol does not move or change the energy you contain any more than painting a picture could create the terrain for you to plant a tree in.

This fifth fact is our first and most crucial place to introduce change. The Human Energy Systems of tomorrow will get us back to our core energy and understanding the needs that are genuinely our own.

To this end, these are the ethics of energy containment that you should follow to maintain good energetic hygiene and begin to return to your energetic authenticity.

Respect Others. Every action made within a culture simply reacts to someone else's needs. We can show better respect for the needs of others by neither encouraging nor deterring another's experience. Listen carefully and deeply, asking questions instead of stating assumptions. Let go of the need to control what other people experience. Allow others to own their experience fully. We cannot give them our experiences, and we cannot have their experience for them. We allow others to experience their own needs fully.

Respect Yourself. This is your life, your chance to explore and expand who you are at an energetic level. These moments here now can never come again. Consider time as a holy thing, where you get to manifest your energy into the physical world. Forgive the energy that has been attached to memory and start from where you are, now. Respect the energy that has brought you to this moment and embrace the direct experience, knowing you are constantly creating it for yourself.

With these two elementary ethics, you can put your energy first. Your health, wellbeing, and growth become a part of every action you take and every movement, no matter how small, becomes a compounding benefit to your life.

Remember, life's events are not a story written to amuse or excite others. Real-life is not limited to a hero's journey. From this base of respect for yourself and others, you begin to create proper actions not based on someone else's reaction.

Handy References

Natural Law in Energy Architecture
1: Energy attaches to Memory.
2: Memories are grouped into Energetic Phases.
3: Phases are energetically isolated.
4: No energetic structure can grow beyond the energies supporting it.
5: Feeling energy does not change the structure of consciousness.

First Principles of Energy Architecture & Engineering

1: <u>Respect all Experiences</u>. Architects build the space for others to have an expansive experience. We do not give them our experiences, nor do we tell them how they should have their own experiences.
- Neither struggle against nor fully surrender to the energy you feel.

2: <u>Set aside the needs of the ego</u> to begin working with the gravitational forces that direct the ebb and flow of awareness.
- Neither encourage nor deter the energy of memory in these experiences.

3: <u>Remember that feeling energy changes nothing.</u> Nothing in your consciousness will evolve if you only feel the energy. To evolve, you must learn to contain that energy: become that energy and act from that energy in the world.
- The energy you feel in your awareness is the energy you are preparing to contain. Proceed in understanding at all times.

Lesson 1: Learning How to Listen to Energy

No matter which path you have tread to arrive at this moment, remember that we all start from where we are now. This is a time for new beginnings and elevating principles. Your horizon expands from here.

My personal goal for Energy Architecture is to help people discover their authentic Self from the conditioning of the needs of others. I would love to see Engineers and Architects designing the most optimally personalized plan for living in Fractal Consciousness and expressing their energetic presence to the fullest degree in the manifest world. Energy Engineering, where we begin this work, is about learning how to discover and administrate the changes to achieve that plan for Fractal Consciousness.

We each are individually responsible for the day-to-day operations that feed into this cycle of continuous self-improvement, self-manifestation, and personal growth.

No one arrives here by accident. There is a path you have taken, that has led you to this moment. This is where we begin this instruction. Learning the processes that govern how you generate your experience of reality is the foundation to becoming an Energy Engineer, and eventually, an Architect.

However, this world of Engineers and Architects doesn't quite exist yet. It's something you and I will create, together. Let's take a moment to get a clear view of the terrain that we will be creating from. I call this terrain 'Manifest Reality' and it is the full sum of the world that your senses can interact with. Manifest Reality is not just the sensory information, but also the ideas and symbols that we form about the information our senses convey to us in this terrain. These symbols manifest as dreams and stories. If you'll recall, 'Energy attaches to memory', and these symbols inform our senses on what state of consciousness to arrange itself into. This energy exchange happens not just in our physical environment, but also with every conversation you have with other people. Let's explore how this happens in closer detail.

The world as it exists today is a collective consciousness that governs the 'acceptable' intervals of awareness through rituals of communication. That is to say; we collectively attain specific levels of consciousness in ritual acts with one another. Have you ever noticed your awareness suddenly changing when someone says, "Good morning!"? Can you feel your attention rearranging itself to answer with an expected reply? This is a ritual of communication that brings all participants to a collectively acceptable level of consciousness. After all, how many of us genuinely answer "How are you?" honestly and fully?

This ritual of communication is the basis for all linear consciousness. It exists on linear timelines that leap sideways at any given moment, like a dream suddenly changing mid-thought. Have you ever noticed how unnatural that can feel? The language we use, and the rituals to convey our level of consciousness are a limitation on our awareness; a limit of the totality of Self that we are capable of bringing into manifest reality.

To begin your first steps into Energy Architecture and Engineering in earnest, you will learn how to become very familiar with the horizon of your inner universe. You will learn how to survey and map your inner universe. This map is the landscape that will become your Architecture plan. In this is a lesson you will create the first part of a blueprint to a new level of consciousness. The Engineer always goes first, and we do not work on anyone for anything we would not go through ourselves first.

The process we will use to map the landscape of your inner universe begins with your beliefs. Look at how you step into each moment, listen to what you tell yourself about that experience. Does it sound something like "I am afraid"? Or maybe "I am in control."? Observe how you understand the world around you and how you choose to respond to it. The fastest way to explore these "I am" statements is to explore your core beliefs. These are some questions I like to use to help me quickly discover who "I am" in this moment.

24

Record your core beliefs:
What morals guide my actions? (eg: what is a sin? What is a virtue?)
What principle should I never neglect?
What do I value in myself?
What do I love in others?

Critically look at your core beliefs, values, and your inner senses' baseline. Be prepared to take actions to align with your core beliefs and values in the following lessons.

To begin your first map, start with a blank sheet of paper. At the top, write "I am…" and complete it with a core belief you've identified above. For now, keep it to a single word. This practice will help you immensely by examining where you might have a division. For example, if your "I am…" statement sounds something like "I am a natural leader when problems arise at work", you'll want to examine why you're thinking of being at work. Is that where you are, right now? Reducing this to a single word can help you become grounded and present in your terrain, your Manifest Reality.

Now that we have a name for the configuration of the horizon in our inner universe, let's review some of the different kinds of 'Human Energy Systems' that create pinpoints within this horizon and how we use them in the formation and development of this inner universe. I would like to recognize that the foundations of my knowledge in these spaces come from a lifetime of studies in these respective cultures, religions, and practices. Please be aware that I have taken liberties with some of the definitions of these deeply cultural spiritual practices, for which no offense or misuse is intended. These are by no means universal definitions, and I do not proclaim myself to be an expert or master on these topics. My gratitude for the knowledge and wisdom they represent is immense.

What follows is a brief summary of the most common energy systems we all use, with more in-depth explanations to follow. Our three primary energy systems are:

- <u>Chi/Qi</u> – Life Force Energy is generated by the food you eat and the air you breathe, which becomes heat of the body, creating a quality of movement and physical strength.
- <u>Shen</u> – meaning 'deity,' 'shimmer,' or 'future mind,' is used in this context: the state of Chi/Qi, having been observed or physically experienced, is transmuted into 'light,' and stored as memory, the foundation of the inner hologram.
- <u>Prana</u> – Shen energy replaying in the body as it becomes actively remembered, generating layers of the aura and chakra energy points. This layer is the filter through which fresh Chi/Qi is observed and attached to memory as Shen.

It is critical to become deeply familiar with each layer of energy, not just in how it feels but in how it moves throughout the dimensions of your awareness.

The Basics of Chi

Let's begin with some basic chi exercises. Start by taking a few deep breaths through your nostrils. The air should fill your lungs, with your belly expanding outward on the inhale, contracting inwards on the exhale. Be sure to keep your diaphragm rested and as still as possible. It can help make sure that your waistband or belt is loose during this exercise.

Continue to focus on your belly during this breathing for a few minutes, then begin to expand your awareness to physical sensations in your body: hot spots, cold spots, tingling spots, and placid spots. When you have a place that feels one of these sensations consistently after several breaths, you will have located the objective of this exercise. If you have never worked with chi before, burping and mild shaking are expected at this stage. A warm sweater or blanket can be handy!

Take a deeper breath into your belly. Feel the sensations as they run from your nostrils, under your brain, down your throat, and into your stomach. Feel the swelling and heat of your vital energy. On the exhale, push that energy consciously to the objective you located. Pay attention to all physical sensations, memories, emotions, and thoughts that arise. Allow the energy to move around this space for a few breaths, then on the inhale, draw that energy back down into your belly. Always finish your energy work with this final step to recover the energy expended in this exercise. Afterward, write down the sensation type, location, and what happened when you moved your energetic presence to that location.

The more you work with this energy, the stronger it will get. You can also gather energy from natural sources like breathing fresh air, consuming fresh produce, or pulling in the energy through your hands. We do not draw energy directly from other living beings, as this is stealing. If you are interested in learning different methods of Chi exercises, I strongly recommend taking up practices like Tai Chi or Qi Gong.

The Basics of Shen

Now that we have an essential experience of chi, we can move into the **'shen'** layer of energy.

Take a moment to review what you recorded from the chi exercise, specifically any memories or daydreams that came up for you. If you can recall that memory now; settle into it like you would a dream. This memory is your unconscious mind, telling you the story of when it observed your energy changing.

This act of remembering through feeling is accomplished through shen energy. It is a 'silent' energy that is completely different in sensation from chi. You can neither spend nor gather more shen, but the more that shen is used, the hotter your internal awareness will feel. Allowing these daydreams to 'heat up' your inner universe creates a kind of flexibility, a plasticity, that we will use to change the constellations of our horizons.

The key to understanding shen is that energy comes from your ability to pay attention to two things simultaneously: the story your mind is telling you and the physical sensations in your body as the story progresses. You may find that your body is holding the energy in many different configurations, and the story is the map to how, when, and why that configuration changes.

The Basics of Prana

Lastly, we come to the **'prana'** or 'pranic' layer of energy.

Prana in "Human Energy Systems" relates specifically to the layer of energy between your Inner Universe and your Physical Body. This layer translates the chi of your shen out into Manifest Reality.

That's right, this layer is your 'aura'. It is the configuration of the energy you are manifesting from your memories. This layer is the filter of what you send out with your words and deeds, as well as the filter that determines what energy from others you are capable of being aware of.

Let's explore prana more closely.

Take a few deep breaths to step into your chi layer of energy, gathering at your stomach. Feel in your body for another objective, a pranic gate of energy that we will call a 'pranic gate' of energy just over the surface of your skin that stands out to you.

This pranic gate of energy is a part of a story. A story told it how to come to this place and why it should stay here. Speaking with energy from this place shares the pranic gate's configuration with other people, so that they will know how and when to experience it. For now, it's just enough to notice that it's here, and begin to listen to the stories that come up around this energy.

Remember to allow your attention to divide between the story the energy is telling you and how the physical sensations shift within your body.

Now, I want you to focus on one pranic gate in particular with the words you have written at the top of your paper. Notice what you can pay attention to, beyond the memories and physical sensations.

Do certain skills become easier or harder with this pranic gate?

29

Is linear thinking or mathematics more
straightforward in one state?

Are your emotions more pronounced, or less?

Symbols can tie these associations like the 'chakras' of pranic energy; they are the energetic lenses you have tied your experiences to that manifest throughout your energetic bodies. These pranic lenses limit and direct your focus to help you accomplish specific tasks.

The more habituated you are to these **'constellations'** of memories, lenses, and the chi to move physically, the more unconscious they become, and the unconscious associates those memories, actions, and energies into specific **symbols** that become the basis for your dream language.

These dream 'symbols' are the unconscious mind's way of explaining moving from one energy state to the next. This process of the symbol triggering the story to begin to run is a process I've poetically named 'Walking The Moonlit Path". This Moonlit Path is the story our unconscious mind tells us about how it observes our energy changing through the energy layers described above. Each story is a collection of memories, beliefs, ideas, wants, needs, expectations, and feelings.

Becoming aware of the Moonlit Path and how it plays out in your linear experience of reality is foundationally critical to Energy Engineering. It represents the state of your consciousness today, including the building blocks you are actively using to make decisions for your future. Take as much time as you need to become deeply familiar with each layer of energy.

Remember, Energy attaches to Memory.

The body continuously cycles energy by collecting it from digested foods, sunlight, breath, and interacting with other living beings. This energy is spent during physical movement or strong emotion that produces a physical reaction (whether or not you acted on it).

When others observe one person's reactions, the energy they project along with a subconscious symbol is stored in the observer's memory. Each observer might store the energy in different octaves and configuration, depending on the pranic gates created by their focus. As that memory is triggered, whether intentionally or not, the initial band of energy is transmitted out from the chi of the physical body, translated through shen as a 'story', and acted on through pranic gates into Manifest Reality.

This continuous cycle of energy and memory is how the energy structure of cultures and subcultures are defined, maintained, and transmitted between individuals.

This is Linear Consciousness.

I would like for you to take a little time this week to begin a meditation practice designed to open up and gently stretch your sensitivity to energy. Start by setting aside 10 minutes where you will not be disturbed in a place where you can sit comfortably. I recommend that if you are using music in the background, try to avoid choosing songs with spoken lyrics.

***

Before we begin this meditation, let's take a moment to make sure any belts or compressing garments are loosened and distracting jewelry removed. Uncross your arms and your legs, with your feet flat on the floor and hands resting gently on your legs.

Remember that at any time, if you need to awaken from your meditation for any reason, you can do so by counting up from 1, 2, 3, taking a deep breath in and open your eyes; feeling energized and fully aware.

We begin by taking a moment to connect within, to that steady rhythm that is your constant companion.

To the beating of your heart.

This rhythmic pulse that can gently lift you, and carry you.

Connected to your pulse, allow your awareness to center in your chest.

As you become aware of any sensations here, take a gentle breath in and allow the sensations to move.

All sensations move in time.

Just for right now, we can allow the sensations to move.

One breath at a time, take as many breaths as you need, for the sensations to become a gentle rhythm.

Breathing in, all the way in. Every layer in.

Breathing out, comfortably out. Every layer interconnected.

Each breath, expanding the sensation of this gentle rhythm, this sphere of tranquil motion.

Until the top of the sphere rests just over the roof of your mouth.

Allowing your tongue to connect to this space, allow yourself to swallow and feel your jaw relax.

Becoming aware of this space of mind, just over the roof of your mouth.

Allowing any sensations to move.

Breathing into the cycles of flowing energy, in the body, in the heart, in the mind.

Flowing together. Filling your body with this pleasant sensation.

Out from you this pleasant sensation travels.

Into and through all dimensions of every multiverse

that makes up the totality of the real you

and all of the energies that have ever built your state of consciousness

Connected to this pleasant energy

Now immediately returns to you, filling all of you, connecting all of you.
The full you. The real you.

The energy of you. The gravity of you.

You may feel sensations like surrender, or maybe some have tensions.

It's okay to feel, and to breathe deep into these feelings.

Softening and relaxing into a totality of self.

Just for right now, you don't really need to be aware of these many dimensions of reality.

You could remember them at any time, couldn't you?

Just for right now, you find yourself in the center of your vast, multidimensional reality.

You are Center of Center.

And as you take another deep breath in, you might just begin to be aware

of this center between the two hemispheres of your mind.

You might begin to notice the space above the roof of your mouth buzzing.

Maybe the breath you take in pulls you deeper into this center of center.

Between the logical and the creative.

Between the right side and the left side.

Between the past and the future.

Breathing into the Center of Center.

Inhaling into the Fractal of the Now, like a golden filament, connecting the hemispheres of your mind.

Allowing this pleasant sensation to pulse out of the golden filament.

Breathing into the Center of Center.

And with one more deep breath

All of your Center of Center rests on that golden filament,

Between the two hemispheres of your mind.

Breathing into this space for as long as you feel comfortable to do so.

And when you are ready to emerge back into reality

Completely centered and aware.

Fully present energized.

Wiggling your fingers, wiggling your toes

Breathing everything that needs to come back with you into manifest reality

From beyond space and time

And opening your eyes, now.

***

Weekly Integration Project 1

Besides meditating, your goal for this week is to identify and map ten symbols and at least 2 Constellations.

To map a constellation:
Start with a single "I am…" belief at the top of the page. Then, over this page and two other pages, draw an outline of yourself, one outline on a clean page.

Each outline gets a label: Chi, Shen, and Prana.

With the "I am" statement clearly in your mind, begin to draw on the outline what you feel, and where. It might be useful to pick different colors and symbols to represent the different states and energy sensations. Make sure to note them in a key on the side.

Mark on these any areas you feel sensations:

The Chi map should include flows or blocks, with a word or symbol describing the sensation of the energy: hot or cold, static, or heavy, etc. Remember to finish all energy work by breathing in your chi into your belly. You will be expected to remember this on your own going forward.

Shen should include single words as a symbol that describes the memories, emotions, and daydreams.

The Prana map should come with words as a symbol indicating what skills or aspects of awareness are pronounced when this constellation is active and where that activity occurs within your physical body.

The combination of these three maps represents a constellation. It is the configuration the multidimensional layers of your body holds itself in to achieve the "I am" state of consciousness and some of the story that this state uses to achieve and maintain this level of consciousness for yourself and those you interact with.

During this week, I want you to ponder the depth and breadth of an expansive thought: "The words you speak become the level of consciousness others will meet you at."

Lesson 2: Understanding the Language of Energy

This Engineering lesson is the first tool necessary to be proficient in creating your experience of reality at an energetic level. It represents a different way to orchestrate the energies described in Lesson 1. It will change the way you know yourself, how you build the lenses of your reality, and the way that you hold the balances of your inner universe within the multidimensional reality you are a part of.

This is the multidimensional language of energy.

Can you remember the pleasant sensation from the meditation last week? This sensation is the energetic foundation of Fractal Consciousness. Let's refer to this collection of sensation and movement as your Inner Hologram.

Before I further explore what the multidimensional language of energy means, I want to offer you another apple. Take a moment to grasp a sense of this apple within your inner universe. You can ask yourself:

What does this apple look like? Smell like? Taste like?
What is it made out of?
Where have you seen this before?
What memories or emotions come up with this apple?

It's not really an apple, is it?

It's more like a hologram, made up of the energy of your memories and emotions attached throughout your lifetime. Your unconscious mind knows the dream symbol of the apple and connects your awareness to every answer you had in those questions above.

This apple is the construct of energy portals in your Inner Universe, spanning across space and time, and the energy you are feeling in every layer of sensation in this constellation (the Chi, Shen, and Prana) is a part of those portals. Your awareness bridges to those moments in time when you physically experienced them and where you actively remembered that experience across your lifetime.

Take a moment to intensely focus on your apple and all of the different times you've remembered one specific experience of 'apple.' Maybe your apple wasn't a kind that you eat. Maybe it was a refrigerator magnet, or a brand of computer, or a poster in an elementary school classroom.

Can you remember those memories individually? Can you notice the presence of your Future Self, paying attention to that moment? Can you now notice your future Self, remembering THIS moment? If you can hold these layers of awareness in parallel, you might just begin to feel a tingling in your mind, a presence, and a sense of pressure. Over time, you may even begin to experience intuitive knowledge with this presence.

This is the multidimensional energy you will learn to work within Energy Architecture and Engineering. The things you can know in the space of this holographic energy can be vastly expansive.

Still, the energy and the awareness that it creates tends to fade, as it collapses into your pranic field and becomes filtered by your active constellations. Throughout Energy Architecture and Engineering, you will learn to collapse and tune your lenses to allow longer, louder, and more powerful moments communing with your multidimensional energy.

Where this hologram of the inner universe exists, you exist multidimensionally.

This hologram holds the consciousness that bridges together every possible lens and thread of energy in every dimension that you are capable of containing. These fields can be broadly categorized in terms like Earthly, telluric, chthonic, galactic, celestial, quantum, and countless more. This hologram exists extra-dimensionally, beyond space and time. The part of you exists beyond everything that you can energetically experience.

Yes, that means there is more to your life than what you are experiencing.

40

In order to connect deeper to this lesson in understanding the language of energy, let's explore a little more of this holographic space, our Inner Hologram, in meditation.

As before, before we begin this meditation, let's take a moment to make sure any belts or compressing garments are loosened and distracting jewelry removed. Uncross your arms and your legs, with your feet flat on the floor and hands resting gently on your legs.

Remember that at any time, if you need to awaken from your meditation for any reason, you can do so by counting up from 1, 2, 3, taking a deep breath in and open your eyes; feeling energized and fully aware.

Taking a moment to breathe in deep and soften into your body.

Connect to the beating of your heart.

Feeling the rhythmic pulse with each breath, remembering gentle rhythm of sensations.

Sensations that are expanding your sphere to the space of mind,

Just over the roof of your mouth.

Remembering the energy of connecting you to the Center of Center:

Between the logical and the creative.

Between the right side and the left side.

Between the past and the future.

Breathing into the Center of Center.

Radiating from that Golden Filament

Breathing in gentle rhythms.

And I want to remind you of something important.

Our multiverse is vast.

Beyond the space between stars, all the way down to the space between atoms.

And from the stars to our cells,

This space is full of tension, and life.

Gravity exists in all of these things.

Gravity exists in all of you.

You are a singularity of consciousness.

Vast beyond this human experience.

Beyond the beyond, is the totality of you,

Connecting now in this moment, in time.

And if you are ready

You can allow your gravity to shift into your Center

Opening to the energy of your reality

And allow the energy of your full self to come forward now.

For just a moment, I want you to breathe in this energy

Gently radiating out from the center of your mind.

Follow the sensations your energy is making

In your nerves, your muscles, your fluids, and your bones.

Let the energy seep into your tissues

And each beat of your heart.

Bringing alignment to every cell in your physical body.

And when you are ready, I wonder if your unconscious mind can help to show you how to step into your holographic space

In the most natural way for you.

Count down from 3, and when you reach 1, you will step between all dimensions

Emerging into your holographic dimension, beyond space and time.

> Three - Gravity beginning to radiate from a golden filament between the hemispheres of your mind.

> Two - Gravity aligning and unifying the left and the right. The past and the future. The above and the below.

> And fully stepping into your Hologram of Inner Universe - ONE.

Taking a moment to notice anything around you.

Images or symbols. Colors or sounds.

Aspects of self or memories that may be playing out.

Make a note of what is active in your hologram,

And if you want to,

you can come back to them whenever you feel called to in the future.

Because, for our entire human lives,

Ae have allowed this holographic space to be fed from unconscious sources.

Now, you have ability to step into the full container of your consciousness.

To access any energy from any dimension that you contain.

Access to the memories of your past,

And beginning to notice the gravity that flows from your Future Self.

Remembering and creating this moment of your eternal Now.

Testing Holograms

In a moment, you will begin to connect your mind to the language of this Holographic Space: the dream language of energy. But before we bring in the language of energy, I wonder what it would be like to allow everything within your hologram to enter a gentle silence?

All of the active energies fading into a gentle darkness, like the moment just before sleep.

And I wonder if your unconscious mind can bring forward to you a hologram of your chi energy.

Allowing it to fade in from the darkness, sitting with this hologram of your chi for just a moment.

And I don't know if you are seeing a map of energy flowing over a hologram of your physical body.

It could have colorful spots where energy is active, or stagnant.

However, this hologram of chi presents to you, it's okay if you want to note what you see.

You can remember it later, if you really wanted to, couldn't you?

You see, these colors and sensations are all a part of your unconscious mind's dictionary.

Symbols attached to energy across space and time.

Each symbol tells a story of how your unconscious mind observes your energy changing over time.

In this holographic space, in the center of center, the totality of all the energy of you is open to you, now.

You can access this holographic space at any time by stepping into the pleasant sensation between the left and the right, the past and the future, into the Center of Center.

You will remember with perfect clarity, everything you need to bring into your manifest, human experience from this holographic space.

And with one more deep breath in all of your Center of Center rests on that golden filament, between the two hemispheres of your mind.

Wiggling your fingers, wiggling your toes,

Breathing everything that needs to come back with you into manifest reality

From beyond space and time.

This week, I want you to settle into this holographic space. Notice what it does when you're having a conversation, cooking a meal, daydreaming, or going about your day. Notice the different stages of energy and pay attention to how they feel.

Can you sense when a memory triggers Chi/Qi to gather in one spot of your physical body when you do simple tasks like preparing a meal or cleaning something in your home?

Can you feel your prana shifting your aura when a person enters the room or when you pass a stranger in the grocery store?

Hold nothing back from your awareness in this holographic space: it is the container of your total consciousness. Allow your mind to wander without getting lost in the wanderings.

Feel how this space of the inner universe brings up the Shen energy you have attached to memory as a single symbol as we have already done with 'apples.'

Focus on using dream language on the symbols and where their energy is stored in your physical body. Start to map the symbols and see if any correlate with the map of the inner universe you started in Lesson 1.

Pay attention to what these symbols mean in context to how you feel about them and where they are in relation to other symbols.

Remember, Memories are grouped in Energetic Phases.

The symbols attached to the energy group by the same energetic type, regardless of what would logically be associated. These groups of interconnected symbols can be referred to as phases.
An example of an energy attached symbol is 'Apple.' In this context, the definition of a 'phase' would be the memories you recalled of apples you have eaten. Separated from this phase would be the experiences apples you have not eaten (pictures, decorations, brands, etc.) in different phases.

Do you recall earlier when you were asked about your specific apple? If you walked a moonlit path with this question, actively remembered energies would be 'manifest' in your aura, creating the lens of your perception. The energy from the memory of eating a specific apple would be present in your aura.

However, the examples that you did not remember represents 'unmanifest' energy that you contain but are not actively using. In Energy Engineering, we are most concerned with the two basic phases that energy can exist in: the Manifest and the Unmanifest.

Manifest Energy is the memory that defines the scope of your awareness and limits your possible reactions. Unmanifest Energy is the energy of every experience you have ever had and are not actively remembering.

In the same way that the mind collects manifest and unmanifest symbols in phases, cultures gather and express their potential experiences from people as a collective consciousness. The universe loves fractals!

Weekly Integration Project 2

Continue your practice of mapping constellations, with your first goal being to map two more constellations. Be sure to begin each session by stepping into your holographic space of the inner universe, where the energies of memory begin to overlap.

In addition, begin keeping a list of the names of symbols that come up for you in your constellations. Remember to narrow them down to single words. You will need this dictionary of symbols to help you begin to translate the more profound languages of your energy.

Dream Language Dictionary Entry Checklist:
- Where did the energy attach to memory?
- What can I remember in this constellation? What dream symbols come up for me?
- What are my wants or needs when I feel these symbols?
- What does having this want or need give me? What could its presence allow me to avoid?

Start looking for symbols that contain the same definitions in different constellations. An example we have already covered would be the word "eating". "Eating" tells us to do the same energetic activity whether we're masticating food or devouring a good book, and can exist in different places on the constellation while still providing the same energetic reactions.

You will require at least one of these symbols specific to your "I am" statement in the later lessons. Be sure to circle it when it comes up in your constellation map. Now review your core beliefs captured from Lesson 1. Can you find any symbols that match a core belief by definition? How about just by feeling?

The expansive thoughts to consider this week are: "Have you begun to identify your dominant constellation yet? What could that mean for the level of consciousness you are presenting for others to meet you at?"

Lesson 3: Conversations in Energy

By now, you're probably beginning to notice that your constellations change. The statements you use for "I am" are rarely universal, and out of necessity, change in context to where you are and whom you are with. This is a normal and natural habit we all have in Linear Consciousness.

With the map filled out in Lesson 2, we can now begin to see the constellation of our awareness at this moment in time.

The layers of physical energy that we act with translate through and being filtered the lenses of pranic energy, attached to memory, and anchored within the physical body balanced on the tip of your awareness. As an Engineer, you will become proficient in mastering that pranic lens and the processes that allow new energies into your awareness. To do so, we need to make an ally of your unconscious mind, for it can help you access the totality of your full awareness.

I want to take a moment to remind you that the universe loves fractals.

Once upon a time, you began as a division between egg and sperm, made whole and singular. You underwent cellular division to grow in complexity until the unity you shared with your biological mother was divided, and you were born. There, you grew as your cells divide, both in your body and in your awareness.

The patterns we continue to follow, these moments of containment and division operating within more expansive octaves as we grow and contain more complexity. As fully formed adults, we explore places within our inner universe where we have divided an awareness to experience the more profound complexity of reality.

It makes me wonder, if I grow to contain the right kinds of experiences, will my following form after this life be more complex?

As before, before we begin this meditation, let's take a moment to make sure any belts or compressing garments are loosened and distracting jewelry removed. Uncross your arms and your legs, with your feet flat on the floor and hands resting gently on your legs.

Remember that at any time, if you need to awaken from your meditation for any reason, you can do so by counting up from 1, 2, 3, taking a deep breath in and open your eyes; feeling energized and fully aware.

Taking a moment to breathe in deep and soften into your body.

Connect to the beating of your heart.

Feeling the rhythmic pulse with each breath, remembering gentle rhythm of sensations.

Sensations that are expanding your sphere to the space of mind,

Just over the roof of your mouth.

Remembering the energy of connecting you to the Center of Center:

Inhaling into the Fractal Now, like a golden filament

Connecting between dimensions of reality.

Between the logical and the creative.

Between the right side and the left side.

Between the past and the future.

Breathing into the Center of Center.

Radiating from that Golden Filament

Breathing in gentle rhythms.

And in a moment, as your unconscious mind begins to prepare

To step through to the Inner Hologram

you can begin to count down

From 3, and when you reach 1, you will step between all dimensions.

Emerging into your holographic container, beyond space and time.

Three - Gravity beginning to radiate from a golden filament between the hemispheres of of your mind.

Two - Gravity aligning and unifying the left and the right. The past and the future. The above and the below.

And fully stepping into your Hologram of Inner Universe - ONE.

Welcome, to the Hologram of Inner Universe

In a moment, we will begin to connect your mind

To the language of the Universe, the language of energy.

But before we bring in the language of energy,

I wonder what it would be like

To allow everything within your hologram to enter a gentle silence

All of the active energies fading into a gentle darkness,

Like the moment just before sleep.

And I wonder if your unconscious mind

Can bring forward to you a hologram of the core belief

Most relevant to you right now.

This core belief says "I am..."

Allow it to fade in from the vastness of your Unmanifest Void,

The Constellation of this Core belief that Says, "I Am...".

Allow your mind to begin to notice

Any memories that begin to play out

The shen energy light of consciousness

And how it changes

How YOU hold your awareness

The balance of your gravity, the flow of your inner energies

Symbols attached to energy across space and time.

Each symbol that stands out from these memories,

Each symbol of energy, sensation, and emotion,

Tells a story of how your unconscious mind,

Observes your energy changing over time.

In this holographic space, in the center of center,

The totality of all the energy of you is open to you, now.

And yet, there is more to this space,

Than what you are able to experience.

Between each line of your constellation,

Behind every molecule of color and sensation,

Is an infinite void

Of all things unremembered.

Where the hologram exists

is only the tip of a multi-dimensional iceberg

Behind which

Is your Fractal Reality.

Breathing into this dimension,

Allowing this expansion of space,

To hold all of you,

Now.

Now, let's ease back into our multidimensional hologram. Feel what is held in your mind and all those symbols they become. Feel the layers of chi flowing through your physical body. Observe how it triggers action by the shen of your memories, how your focus is the prana that holds the memory in place. These are bridges between the manifest and the unmanifest layers of reality, the layer between the inner universe and the outer.

Every memory I am not recalling, for every thread of energy I have ever contained but am <u>not</u> actively using, these are housed in the realm of the unconscious mind that we can call the Unmanifest Void. This inner hologram contains the many dimensions of reality; my energy, sensory experiences, and memories. Yet, there is another part of you outside and totally beyond the sensations of the inner universe.

The energy you remember creates the lens of your perception. But there is more to this life than what is being experienced. While energy is attached to memory, the un-remembered energy rests in the Unmanifest Void. This void contains all that you have ever experienced and are not actively remembering. When you think of an apple, who decides which of those memories manifest into your prana?

There is the touch of a Decider behind every thought that you have, which leads to a physical response. When you thought of an apple in the previous lesson, could you feel your Decider exploring every energy attached to every memory in the span shorter than a heartbeat? Could you feel the energy lift out of your unconscious mind as those portals activate and the hologram floods with sensation?

Your Decider is the part of your Self who is responsible for choosing the memories your consciousness needs to experience to grow in complexity. It is the deciding force behind how you hold your energy and the layers of pranic lensing that slows and filters the energies of reality, creating opportunities to explore who you are beyond the confines of linear consciousness.

Your Decider has access to all of your energy, manifest and unmanifest. It has experienced every memory you have ever contained, and it selects the energy you use to create your internal experiences. This Decider is the co-creator of your inner universe.

Some people experience an adverse sensation when they realize there is a Decider between the ego and the fast ocean of memory they contain. Remember that the Decider is your ally, just like the unconscious portions of your mind that regulate your body temperature, breathing, and heart rate. They have held these functions for you in service to the collective, multidimensional being that you are, and will continue to do so from each lifetime's conception to its cessation.

As you begin to pay attention to your dreams/daydreams and the language it represents, your Decider may engage you more strongly. It knows when you are paying attention and will respond in kind. I would like for you to spend this next week learning to hear your Decider, to notice how it brings up the experience of your inner universe in dream language, and begin the process of trusting this aspect of your Self.

It's essential to be clear that in this space of the inner universe, the energy you can feel changes nothing about your "level of consciousness". To expand your consciousness as an Energy Engineer, you learn to master your divisions, to contain how and when you create your energy beyond the confines of linear consciousness. The tension between these divisions creates the energy from which you can act. This is the most significant difference between the linear and the Fractal: linear depends on an external experience to determine how you divide your awareness to generate the energy of your reality.

Being in fractal consciousness means holding multiple constellations together consciously to provide a service of expanded consciousness to the world. It means that who you are is no longer governed by the energy within the actions of others.

Respect is ensuring that the divisions you are calling into a direct experience for your personal growth are not being given to others in ways that override their own needs of consciousness. In this way, while stepping into your most authentic and complete Self at an energetic level, you begin to hold the space for others to step into their own authenticity.

Remember, Phases are Energetically Isolated.

Phases are expressed as organically generated fractal structures of consciousness. Bear with me here; I know that's a big one. One phase will flow into the next phase by using symbols containing energy that simultaneously bridges many phases. Let's look at how these manifests in daily life: identifying a need to buy groceries.

Let's consider your pantry as an aspect of consciousness. It is a dimension of space for the need of 'hunger' to exist. Your pantry is low, so you identify a need for more groceries and make a decision to start getting these groceries now. You write down a list of symbols based on how they previously made you feel. You take your list with you in your vehicle to purchase the items.
You enter the store, identify, select your appropriate items, pay for them, and return home. You array the new things in your pantry based on habit, memory, or convenience and decide the need to obtain groceries has been met.

Most of these actions are examples of monophasic awareness. You would not usually think of using your turn signal or paying bus fare while writing your grocery list. Likewise, you would probably not be considering which check stand to use when parking your car or fishing for your house keys in front of the front door with an armload of groceries.

Now we can see that 'apple' in this context can be an 'interphasic' symbol, as it exists as on your list and an object to interact with physically. The apple magnet on your fridge might have reminded you that you need to get groceries. Interphasic symbols bridge energetic phases. This is how a symbol can help the mind traverse its fractal structures of direct experience using memory and energy.

Weekly Integration Project 3

I hope you've become comfortable with the process of mapping constellations by now! I want you to map another two constellations this week. Dig deep and be willing to explore the less comfortable symbols.

Begin to draw lines between symbols that feel like they have the same energy sensations at the chi layer, using the same color codes in your keys. Have you found any symbols that match your core beliefs?

The project for this week is all about learning to identify unmanifest energy.

Examine what happens in your Inner Universe when you mentally shift from one symbol to another, which does not have a common point of chi or shen connection between them.

What happens to your daydreams and memories when you attempt to bring up these two symbols simultaneously?
What happens to your pranic lenses? Do they become more active or less active?

When you've found a set of symbols that create a significant silence in your awareness, I want you to 'Walk a Moonlit Path' between these two symbols. Allow your daydreams to fill in the blanks for telling the story of how your energy is changing between these two points. Make notes afterward about what symbols stood out to you, any sensations of resistance or discomfort, and where they were located. Try to drill into what physical senses were at play in this experience.
The expansive thought this week is: "What more could there be to consciousness if there is more to this life than what you are experiencing?"

Lesson 4: Asking Questions and Understanding Answers

I would like to start this lesson out by reminding each of us that, because we are born into a physical body and are capable of physically exist in the world, the actions we take in this world will ripple out touch the end of time. Becoming our authentic multidimensional Self allows us to step into this profound truth with all that we are. If we do not, the only thing that will touch the end of forever will be the parts of other people's authenticity we have repeated for ourselves.

By stepping into the hologram of your consciousness, you have begun to exercise the mental muscles needed to begin bridging new constellations from across your multiverse. By bridging more of your authentic Self from the unmanifest void and manifesting into reality, you not only release the needs and burdens that do not belong to you, but you also step into the strongest possible constellation that is capable of supporting your energy.

In Linear consciousness, this bridging of the multiverse happens so seamlessly that we've learned to tune out the process. It just feels natural. It only becomes apparent that something unusual happens when an internal lens is pulled out of alignment: an experience begins to loudly repeat itself in different places or with different people. Tones of familiar guides or internal dialogues suddenly change. Rooms in your home or workplace are feeling dark or oppressive. An everyday experience suddenly covering you in chills. These are examples of your unconscious mind translating these shifts into your direct experience.

You see, the brain is a sensory organ like your eyes and ears, skin, and tongue. One of its duties as a sensory organ is to sense energy. Each person maps to their reality based on their senses (some prefer audio, visual, or touch), and these maps unconsciously translate into the speaking style. (Can you hear what I'm singing out to the universe? Do you see my point? How does that feel to you? Have you caught the senses I use in these questions?)

Suppose we narrow down to one of these senses, like visual. In visual memories, we have a full scope of powerful memories and dream symbols translate their energies to use as your first engineering project. This project will explore how to bridge what you can physically see in our reality and what you can imagine through the process of visualization. Please note that we are using elements of hypnotic positive hallucination in order to turn up the volume of normally subtle patterns.

If you have unresolved trauma or begin to experience symptoms of emotional crisis at any time during this exercise, please stop immediately and seek assistance from the healing practice or modality of your preference. I do not suggest you move forward with this exercise until you have regained authority over your internal state.

That being said, through training with your Decider, you can develop a level of deep trust in the energy you are manifesting into your experience.

Using the same method as the previous meditations, breathe into the sphere and connect with your Center of Center. Step into your Inner Hologram.

When you feel ready to take the next step, I want you to test the strength of the connection to your Decider.

Ask your Decider to show you a single red line <u>with your eyes closed</u>.

Allow the red line to manifest without an expectation of any specific outcome.

This is your Decider showing you what lenses are currently active in your constellation. Notice the tone of the red line; consider if it has any vividness or dullness. Experience any memories that may come up for you and note them.

Open your eyes and ask your Decider to show you a red line again. Practice bringing forward your unconscious mind into your waking reality. This exercise can develop powerful skills like aura reading, seeing energy flows, and the like. Notice how the red line changes, if at all, across different environments and emotional states. Treat this as a baseline to gauge how your pranic field is creating a lens of awareness and translating your experience of reality.

If the experience of the red line has not produced any variances like changes in color, number of lines, or distracting mental stories or dreams while you have been visualizing this red line, you have maintained what can be called a 'stable phase'. The phase that remains stable throughout the majority of your day is your dominant constellation. Remember not to assign any values or judgments to a constellation. They all served a valuable purpose in your life at some point, and deserve to be stated in the positive.

The energy from memories constructing your hologram in your dominant constellation is static, unchanging, and stable. But what happens to this red line if you try to play a genre of music you don't usually listen to or like? What happens to that red line if you turn on the tv to a drama, news, or romance? How about when talking to a friend or family member? Eventually, you'll come up against an environment that drastically changes how you see the red line. When you do, you'll have an example of a different 'phase,' a constellation of memories that changes your consciousness based on which phase your Decider has called forward from the unmanifest void.

Stepping into Fractal Consciousness is a vast experience, and you have taken the first step into the Fractal, beyond the foundations, by learning how to hear and understand the language of your energy.

Frequent Questions and Answers:

1. What if the line isn't red? I see an (orange-yellow, purple, pink, green, etc.) line. Does this matter?

    Variances to our expectations in this space are a message from your Decider. You may want to step into your hologram and have a daydream 'conversation' on why the orange-yellow line. Pay attention to the feelings and energies that come up if you try to change the color to red gently. Look/listen carefully at any memories that come up here!

2. When I read your words, I feel like my brain is reorganizing itself or moving and expanding to capture your tones. Is this expected?

    Yes, it is normal to feel your mind rearranging neural pathways to make new connections and expand its sphere of influence.

3. When I read these or practice with the concepts, I focus on galactic or universal environments rather than the environment around me (things in front of me like trees, etc.).

    While exploration into the multiverse can be a beautiful experience, it can also become a trap, where we quickly lose track of our energy and get lost in the story we expect to hear. It is crucial to come back to the physical body and physical experience in these early stages. It will help you maintain a point of connection to the world your body lives in.

4. Do we each pre-define our limit of consciousness in these phases?

The limitation of your awareness is governed by the phases that you are actively using, yes.

5. I see blank spots in dreams or daydreams, or a memory comes up blank.

   Blank spots can happen when a memory or symbol is attached to a Phase that is too far removed from your active awareness; the memories and the energy are 'stuck' in an Unmanifest Void. You can see the same influence of a too-distant Phase with future memory when the phase it comes from is too far out of scope from the phase you interpreted it in. It doesn't mean anything is wrong or needs to be fixed. It is simply that the energy from those phases is not compatible with the energy phase you are actively in.

Remember, no Structure can grow beyond the energies that support it.

Energy is the root of direct experience; it is a tension between the polarities of a divided aspect of awareness. The dividing force is described as a need of consciousness. The needs we have attached to specific symbols determines the level of consciousness that symbol represents in our awareness.

Weekly Integration Project 4

When you ask a question of your Decider, the answer is always a change in consciousness. What you can remember and carry forward from that answer depends on the energies relevant to your active constellations.

We have begun to explore how phases are mapped across our multiverse, each phase containing a pre-defined limit of consciousness based on the energy attached to it. Spend this next week exploring unmanifest phases with your Decider.

For the Integration Project his week, I want you to ask your Decider to show you the symbol you need to work with next.

It will be helpful to review the pranic lenses of your constellations. Map the constellation around this chosen symbol, making special notes for the beliefs and expectations you may have around it. Walk a Moonlit Path for each of the symbols you receive in dream language for this constellation, observing how your awareness grows as you begin to include more previously unmanifest layers.

Once you understand what it feels like to map an unmanifest constellation, I want you to use this process to explore a question that you don't personally know the answer to. This time, you will truncate the mapping process by asking a question to your Decider and Walking the Moonlit Path. Keep your awareness open for the question you don't have the experience, knowledge, or memory to answer. Maybe it's a philosophical question of a moral choice or personal ethic.

By now, you should have a firmly established dictionary of symbols committed to memory to understand not just how the lens of your awareness is changing but to notice in parallel what in your inner hologram needs to change to understand and integrate the answer.

Practice these conversations with your Decider throughout the week, make a point to expect an experience of remembering.

The expansive thought this week is: "How many of these constellations that you have mapped from the previous lessons belong to other people?"

Lesson 5: Thinking in Energy

Over the past four lessons, we have learned how to discover the symbols that create the constellations of our reality and slow down their process as they trigger a movement from one state of awareness into another. We have our ability to recognize the layers of energy systems as they create the hologram of inner universe. In just a few short weeks, you have built the first foundations of Fractal Consciousness.

Our next step is to practice moving from one energetic phase into another seamlessly. Where external factors used to trigger these shifts in "I am" through feelings and symbols, we will now begin to practice moving them from our energy.

We will learn how to bridge the available memories of two constellations together. This mapped bridge is the first step you will take as an Energy Engineer towards making a change in consciousness that is not dependent on a direct physical experience to inform and generate your reality. With this step, you become personally accountable for how our beliefs generate, define, and prioritize your energetic phases.

Let's begin with an essential definition of the structure of belief:

AXIOM
ax·i·om
/ˈaksēəm/
noun
a statement or proposition regarded as being established, accepted, or self-evidently true.
"the axiom that supply equals demand"
Mathematics: a statement or proposition on which an abstractly defined structure is based.
Origin: Greek, "Axios" (worthy)

The hologram of your mind is built on self-defined axioms.

The axioms we build our world with are conceived when an experience presents us with a Decision we are unwilling to make. The axiom forms the phases of your awareness. It condenses into a single line of gravitational thought: a belief about what it means to exist in this phase and why it is imperative to hold the phase in this constellation.

Every axiom that defines your reality is created from a need of consciousness. It is based on one of the three essential Needs of Consciousness: a need to become, do, or remember. The needs that persist the longest are usually the hardest experiences to avoid.

For example, let's say that in your formative childhood, a parent saw behavior from a child that made them uncomfortable: the child needed to be seen as solid and fearsome to protect a boundary; maybe they roared like a lion in a supermarket. The parent recalled how their own parents reacted to this similar situation, and repeated the reaction to the child, telling them to hush and embedding them with the same constellation of suppressing the voices and need for boundaries. The energy attached to the child's memory, and every time that behavior of needing to protect a boundary surfaced within, that constellation would repeat just after it, reminding them to suppress their voice.

An axiom has formed here, a belief that when the need for a boundary arises, it 'should' be followed with an experience of self-suppression. Over the years, these axioms become an unconscious habit that trigger energetic levels in repeating octaves: from home life to school life and work life. On occasion, the axiom can be so firmly embedded that it manifests physically. In the example earlier, maybe the child began to slow down in spelling and vocabulary, or maybe they had a frequent sore throat.

It is crucial to examine where a pattern of injury is repeating. For example, where a frequent ankle injury happens, examine what memories come up in the energy of your ankle. Were you walking to a job you disliked? Where in your life did you form a belief that you needed to slow down?

Can you see how the dream interpretation can translate how the energy of beliefs acts on the physical body now?

I would like to take a moment to recap this at a higher level. So far, an axiom is an external and unconscious adoption of someone else's constellation and the need it was conceived with, which triggers and runs just after a naturally occurring need. The adoption and execution of this foreign need prevent the original need from being met, leaving the individual trapped within the external needs of others and unable to express their consciousness. These often present in our lives as loops of experiences that are full of struggle, and occasionally, trauma.

We have many methods at our disposal to collapse these constellations that create the looping experience of reality. Whichever method you select from the vast array in humanity's toolbox, there are two specific options I want Energy Engineers to be keenly aware of. The first method involves collapsing the original need into the unmanifest void, preventing the triggering constellation from manifesting. This array can be seen in holistic practices from Reiki to Hypnosis, and the view of Energy Architecture and Engineering, largely incomplete in their effectiveness. Proper growth and thriving cannot come from suppressing the needs of consciousness, which brings us to the second method: isolating the experience being avoided and learning how to both uncover and realize the original need.

In this context, these needs of consciousness are your awareness attempting to learn how to express itself in greater complexity. After we have learned how to act on the energy of our original need and not the axioms of others, we can begin to focus on the experiences that expand our awareness to levels beyond our immediate environment.

These aren't just any experiences, but strange experiences. Ones that give you goosebumps or create moving sensations over your mind and heart. These strange experiences are a part of the fractal universe, attempting to grow in complexity through division.

Now that we have examined axioms in the micro, let's zoom out and view them in the macro. As I've mentioned, the universe loves fractals. It is very easy to see how an embryo will divide itself to create more complex forms and functions, and this process does not stop after we are born. Before it was divided into the Manifest and Unmanifest awareness you hold today, the wholeness and completeness of your consciousness take root in physical reality by dividing and subdividing into more complex structures. Where genes activate or grow dormant to express changes throughout your lifetime, so do dream language concepts structures grow and fade. By learning to communicate in the language of the unconscious mind, you make an ally of your unconscious aspects of Self and the axioms by which it generates your experience of reality.

We should all grow keenly aware of unmanifest phases and the beliefs that generate them, as they can severely influence the physical body and vice versa. The same is true of a culture's influence on the individual. The maps to dreams and their subdivided structures are passed from person to person in the same way that genes are passed from ancestors and parents to children.

While the same laws, philosophies, and moral principles of genetics might not apply to how we look at the energetic basis of a culture, it still provides a very similar thread from which we can weave with: the axiom.

What you believe to be necessary for your experience becomes your reality. The gravity with which you hold your consciousness allows it to divide and sub-divide into increasing complexity based on the culture you immerse yourself within. The body and the mind are echoing the Fractal in balanced resonance.

Take a moment to review the Natural Laws of Energy Architecture:
1. Energy attaches to Memory
2. Memories are grouped into dimensional phases
3. Phases are energetically isolated
4. No energetic structure can grow beyond the energies supporting it

5. Feeling energy does not change the structure of consciousness.

When we feel the energy of axioms moving within mind and body, we arere feeling the divided aspects of our consciousness, whose tension is creating our reality through a kind of gravity of consciousness. Feeling energy is a symptom of a change that has already happened, an etheric wind created by shifting your inner phases.

I take a deep breath in and let my awareness expand into all of the phases currently building my reality. I focus on the symbols that my mind is translating. They are like feeling the shifting of inner winds and patiently observing the story my brain is telling me about those shifting winds. They are the code that informs the way I experience reality. The greatest gift I can give myself is the freedom and clarity to ensure these codes are genuinely mine. The consciousness I am attempting to express and grow into is wholly my own.

Being fully aware of my shifting awareness is how I become individually accountable for the beliefs that generate, define, and prioritize my energetic phases.

Remember, feeling energy changes nothing.

The sensation of feeling energy is the mind observing a shift in tension between divided aspects of awareness. The function of the mind, as a sensory organ, includes the sensing of energy. It describes observations using symbols that are energy attached in memory.

Like having a daydream, moving the symbol does not move or change the energy you contain any more than painting a picture could create the terrain for you to plant a tree in.

Energy is contained by directly experiencing energy with the physical body (as compared to the mental, emotional, or spiritual body), free of expectation and storytelling.

These moments of containment are preceded by heightened intuition and synchronicity, so the act of containing energy requires a certain amount of fearlessness. Feeling energy without using it to make an action will repress your growth towards new levels of awareness. Remember that you are always personally accountable for the energy you put into the world.

Weekly Integration Project 5

This week, we will be focusing on feeling energy outside of the usual Linear constraints of consciousness. This process is a little complex, but can simply be described as the energetic process that inspires our ability to have questions and understand answers. A question, at the energetic level, is a request for a change in consciousness. The answer is the way you allow that energy to change you.

What follows is a series of questions designed to tickle your mind. Not your logical mine or your creative mind. Your other mind. Ease into the sensations and answers that come up for you.

Have you ever picked up an object or had an event bring out a sudden moment of clarity that drew in all of your attention, like gravity? Maybe you experienced a strange sensation, like memories that have not happened yet with the object. Maybe it felt like this moment was directly linked to a moment in the future that was so profound, the future you remembered this moment in perfect clarity. What if this was the origin of intuition?

In this dream-like state of overlap, we can capture glimpses of what we will believe in that future moment. We can map the constellations that created this awareness and the symbols that brought us to that moment if we are quick. If it feels like a good moment, we can look for the energy of those symbols in our waking life. If they are negative moments, it can give us warnings about what we may want to avoid or integrate.

This is where Energy Engineering gets strange.

I want you to pick a moment in your life that stands out to you, one where your intuition was clear and powerful. I want you to step into your inner hologram and bridge this moment to that moment in the past. Give your past Self the symbols you will need to understand your decisions at that time.

Afterward, I want you to stay open to receiving a symbol from your future Self. These intuitive handshakes across time will help you to build the trust and the energetic muscles needed to begin working with 'gravity,' the morphoplastic energy structure of consciousness, before it enters reality through a lens of awareness.

The expansive thought of the week is: "Who could you be if you were not reacting from memory?"

Lesson 6: Testing in Reality

By the time you reach this lesson, you should be able to work with your Decider in the hologram of the inner universe to bring forward unmanifest energies. You should know how to define what activity this energy generates within you and move this energy between the manifest and the unmanifest consciously. These energies are potent triggers of manifestation and expansion. By consciously selecting which energies to bring into your reality, you become an engineer of your reality. You can change your inner universe with what you already contain within your consciousness.

As Engineers, we always go first. We do not offer any solutions to others that we ourselves are not willing to experience.

Let's take a moment to review our First Principles of Energy Architecture & Engineering.

1: Respect all Experiences. Architects build the space for others to have an expansive experience. We do not give them our experiences, nor do we tell them how they should have their own experiences. Neither struggle against nor fully surrender to the energy you feel. Stay centered in your balance.

2: Set aside the needs of the ego to begin working with the gravitational forces that direct the ebb and flow of awareness. Neither encourage nor deter the energy of memory in these experiences.

3: Remember that nothing in your consciousness will evolve if you only feel the energy. Feeling energy changes nothing. To evolve, you must learn to contain that energy: become that energy and act from that energy in the world.
The energy you feel in your awareness is the energy you are preparing to contain. Proceed in awareness at all times.

Now, I want to add a few new keys to our multidimensional map of constellations. Not every symbol works the same, as I'm sure you've

78

begun to notice by now. Some symbols can become bridges that shift which constellations become manifest or unmanifest. With this knowledge, we can begin to step into the realm of Energy Architecture, where we move energies that control the flow of chi, shen, and prana within our reality.

These are the definitions of the different types of phases that you should now be at least topically familiar with as an energy engineer:

- A singular active constellation governing energy flow from the inner universe into the outer universe is called a 'monophase' of reality. E.g. Specific Nouns like "Apple PC".
- A symbol that bridges two monophasic symbols in linear motion is defined as an 'interphasic' symbol. E.g. Verbs like "Eating", or "Driving", or "Typing".
- A symbol that bridges between multiple phases simultaneously is a 'multiphasic' symbol. E.g. Homonyms like "Apple", or "Ring".

Please take this time to update your maps now by exploring where the same symbol is used in linear interphase or metaphase. I mark mine out with a dotted circle for interphase and a solid circle for metaphase but use whatever works for you.

By mapping the symbols that are pivotal to the expansion and contraction of your focus, you can now pinpoint and zero in on the deeper beliefs that create your core experience of reality. These symbols are held in place using stories, dream language, and memories to re-create a pattern throughout the octaves of this lifetime continually. In a decade of experience, I have yet to find a challenge to the axiom that this pattern is an experience we would do anything to avoid. I believe that each of us has built an entire personality around avoiding the experience created by a divided aspect of consciousness.

It is the one division we struggle to accept, so we create complexity ad infinitum in every other direction possible. This is where we have used fractal consciousness to create a loop, one that protects us and prevents us from further divisions until we are ready to consciously accept the evolution it represents. These maps you have been creating are all the places you could accept further divisions. Further examination will show you what you have been dancing round.

This is the precipice of true evolution and expansion of your consciousness. Until this point, most of you have been dependent on an external experience to govern how to expand your awareness, so long as it avoided the blank spots in your map. In fractal consciousness, you are free to expand virtually anywhere but to get there, you must be able to contain the division that has kept you in your current state of linear consciousness.

Sometimes that process can feel like death.

Remember to breathe through it. You've been through it before and will go through it again.

This is what Energy Engineering is meant to accomplish: the containment of the divided aspect of awareness through a direct experience to complete the process of fractal consciousness by overcoming the block created by linear consciousness.

I move with the energy of my reality instead of the stories created by the expectations, desires, struggles, and needs.

I align with the gravity of my own needs of consciousness; my actions are in harmony with the energy that I create my reality with. This is how I contain a divided aspect of my awareness that has been trapped into stasis by linear consciousness.

As a process, "containment" means becoming aware of unmanifest energy that I can feel within the lens of my consciousness but do not experience any memories or symbols associated with it. By acting on this unmanifest energy and observing how it manifests in reality, I begin to experience a new layer of my consciousness. Once I have turned this single action into a repeatable habit, I can say that I have fully contained that (previously) unmanifest energy and have manifested more of my total Self into reality.

80

Try it, now. Step within your inner universe and ask your Decider to bring up the unmanifest energy you need to contain to expand your consciousness.

As with all meditations, follow the process of stepping into your Inner Hologram.

In this space, bring up the topic that your Decider has shared to you as the Unmanifest Energy to follow.

Allow your awareness to lean into the sensations of that energy.

Feeling the sensations of your awareness as it shifts.

Becoming aware of the story your mind is telling you about this shifting.

This is following Unmanifest Energy on the Moonlit Path.

Feel whatever comes up and note where this energy travels through in your body. It will give you a hint at the action you need to perform with this energy.

Remember that you are always accountable for every action you take in this world. Look for the most positive expression of your actions. By acting on Unmanifest Energy, you grow one step closer to containing the division that governs your state of consciousness.

Containment is learning to work with the gravity of your consciousness. This gravity is responsible for the expansiveness of your awareness. There is a difference between reacting to unmanifest energy from others and acting on the energy that belongs to your needs.

You can see by your maps that the interphasic symbols are the moment where you have avoided an experience. By mapping enough of these interphasic symbols, you can observe the pattern you are avoiding. Look at the feelings that come up for these symbols, the beliefs you've created around them, and where they land in your body.

Maybe the symbol is 'relationships,' and just like in a dream, the relationship ended in such a way that you were unable to complete an experience. Maybe it was a need to set a boundary, and maybe it was a need to experience vulnerability. Look at where the pattern has repeated and what that moment has allowed you to avoid. That is the aspect of consciousness you are preparing to contain through direct experience.

Our next step is to explore and practice following unmanifest energy. The following meditation will help you establish this practice.

Before we get into the actual containment process, there is a critical factor that needs to be understood if your containment is to be successful. When working with unmanifest energy, it is precarious and easily lost without anchors to shen or pranic lensing. Unmanifest energy exists in the realms of pre-consciousness, and I've taken to calling it morphoplastic (form – shapable) for this reason. Even with advanced meditators and experienced Engineers, morphoplastic structures rarely survive 9 minutes in a manifest energy field before it dissolves or is dropped if the constellation switches suddenly.

Have you ever noticed a daydream suddenly change, stop, or collapse entirely out of memory. It happens when the story running on an unmanifest aspect of consciousness that extended beyond what that unmanifest energy could support. You should aim to complete any containment activities within '9 minutes' of feeling the unmanifest energy. By mapping out and inoculating against interphasic symbols, you can reduce pitfalls and delays.

Without further ado, the process of containment is as follows:

Identify the dominant constellation.
Examine your maps for the interphasic symbols that are hardest to pay attention to. You may notice that your eyes slide over the symbols several times or that thinking about them causes your inner dialogue to go silent or static. On walking a moonlit path, the story changes suddenly when these symbols appear, ultimately dropping the energy structure in most cases. These symbols are closest to the constellation to work with, the dominant constellation creating the gravity of awareness.

The question to ask yourself is:

What Need is creating my reality?

Map interphasic symbols.
Start a new map. Trace together the symbols of your dominant phase, where you struggle and surrender in this state of consciousness. This new map will help you define the polarity and

gather the memories necessary for this constellation. It is often helpful to record any memories, dreams, moonlit paths, symbols, and beliefs discovered through this process.

The first polarity is defined by how you struggle against experiencing the symbols. Look carefully at which symbols you avoid and note them on one side of the polarity. The second polarity is defined by the symbols you surrender to, often without question or conscious consideration.

The question to ask yourself is:

How do I struggle against this Need? How do I surrender to it?

Name the polarities of the divided aspect of consciousness.
Each polarity contains a portion of the gravity of your inner universe. Between these polarities is the tension we have been calling 'energy'. This energy has been the basis for your decisions deeper, more unconscious. Name each polarity with a single word that encapsulates and contains the connective meaning between each symbol in that polarity.

The question to ask yourself is:

How has this served me in the past?

Identify and name the need creating this reality.
This need is the source of repeating unmanifest energy across the many octaves of your experiences. Experiences that you may be avoiding. Name this need with a single word that encapsulates, contains, and describes the experience that it represents. This must remain a single word, as it contains the gravity of both polarities.

The question to ask yourself is:

What is the lesson of this Need?

Calling up the unmanifest energy.

84

To receive the symbols of the need, walk a Moonlit Path to completion within the 9-minute timeframe. Allow this moonlit path to inform your conscious mind how it observes the energy of your awareness changes.

The question to ask yourself is:

What has this story allowed me to avoid?

Act on the unmanifest energy consciously.
In the same way that you called in an experience to solve a problem, call in the unmanifest energy for you to act on in a direct experience. Call your unmanifest aspects of consciousness into direct manifestation.

The question to ask yourself is:

Who am I now that I have understood this lesson?

Understanding the result.
Record on your new map how the symbols have changed. Did they become monophasic? Did they remain interphasic? Have they become metaphasic? Did some change but not others? Where has a change in belief, habit, or energy, changed your energetic lenses at the deepest possible levels? What does this mean for your awareness?

Remember, Respect Others.

Every action made within a culture simply reacts to someone else's needs. We can show better respect for the needs of others by neither encouraging nor deterring another's experience. Listen carefully and deeply, asking questions instead of stating assumptions. <u>Let go of the need to control what other people experience.</u> Allow others to own their experience fully. We cannot give them our experiences, and we cannot have their experience for them. We allow others to experience their own needs fully.

Containing energy changes everything.

The sensation of feeling energy is the mind observing a shift in tension between divided aspects of awareness. The function of the mind, as a sensory organ, includes the sensing of energy. It describes observations using symbols that are energy attached in memory.

Like having a daydream, moving the symbol does not move or change the energy you contain any more than painting a picture could create the terrain for you to plant a tree in.

Energy is contained by directly experiencing energy with the physical body (as compared to the mental, emotional, or spiritual body), free of expectation and storytelling.

These moments of containment are preceded by heightened intuition and synchronicity, so the act of containing energy requires a certain amount of fearlessness. Feeling energy without using it to make an action will repress your growth towards new levels of awareness. Remember that you are always personally accountable for the energy you put into the world.

We can learn most from this fifth fact by understanding that we are trapped in a cycle of reacting to other people's unmanifest energy at a cultural level. This unmanifest energy can look like many things:

A textbook definition
The opinions of others
An overheard conversation
The experience of a fictional character

These contain some energy needed by their original creator, their 'origin,' and passed from person to person, culture to culture, without ever being fully contained. I know it can be a little challenging to grasp initially, with such benign symbols like apples and kitchen pantries. But what happens when you start looking at concepts like 'security' or 'intimacy'? Can you see how a multiphasic symbol like 'money' might become a critical factor between these two? Could you see how the energy you contain about 'money' might suddenly affect what you can or cannot make decisions on when it comes to 'security' or 'intimacy'? Worse, the needs shared by cultures are often adopted by people who don't need them, creating cycles of struggle or surrender that take people far away from their natural energetic growth.

This fifth fact is our first and most crucial place to introduce change. The Human Energy Systems of tomorrow will get us back to our core energy and understanding the needs that are genuinely our own.

To this end, these are the ethics of energy containment that you should follow to maintain good energetic hygiene and begin to return to your core energy.

Weekly Integration Project 6

The integration project for this week is to perform a full containment on your dominant constellation. Take as long as you need on this project. Do not move ahead to the next lesson until you have done so. Remember to keep communicating with your future and past levels of awareness. Let your ever-present-now be the bridge for accomplishing this task. This project is a test of your ability to send gravity through your memories to take a complete step into Fractal Consciousness.

The expansive thought for this week is: To learn a thing is to let it change you. What are you interested in learning? Does it align with how you want to be changed?

Lesson 7: Connecting with Gravity

Fractal Consciousness is a state of consciously creating reality by being centered within your Inner Universe and all the layers of energy that create your reality. At a very technical level, achieving fractal consciousness means that the energy of your thoughts and words contain clarified shen, which in turn creates a new phase of Human Energy: energy like morphoplastic shen that allows the mind to establish connections beyond the linear constrained consciousness created by our modern concepts of language and time. There are many other forms of chi, shen, and prana to explore, and some, you will create for yourself. Imagine what energy systems we can create together!

One such energy system I would like to introduce you to is "Gravity".

The linear words that once told you how to move from one energy state to another, that defined your needs for you, now contains morphoplastic energy and has become a fractal word. These words can present unmanifest energies into other people's consciousness in a way that rapidly increases their containment capacity when used in context to the need's polarities.

Now that you have a memory containing morphoplastic structure in your consciousness, it is embedded within your energy system. It flows with your chi, transmutes into shen, filters into your prana, and is capable of carrying this new energy signature into every octave you are capable of communicating in. It is a word with "Gravity" to it, enabling those with a resonant configuration of prana will pick up on and pay close attention to.

I want to assure you that this does not mean that you are no longer incapable of speaking and thinking in linear consciousness. Speaking from energy means you are using symbols in your communication to change someone's awareness to something more familiar to you or that you are deliberately moderating your awareness to meet someone where they are at in consciousness. The dominant constellation is preserved and navigated interphasically through rituals of communication.

Be sure to pause and give yourself a moment to recalibrate when you hear people speaking from an unresolved need. You might notice how some people can go beyond avoiding their individual needs of consciousness, broadcasting the symbols for that constellation to manifest in the people around them.

These are the people who tend to push off their individual growth to other people, be it peers, children, co-workers, or social acquaintances. You begin to catch the people who push their unresolved needs onto others to see who can work out their problems for them while continuing to avoid the experience they need to expand their awareness. Their words become the level of consciousness that their families, tribes, collective cultures and communities operate from.

While it's essential to observe this when it happens, you cannot pass judgment on this behavior. It is simply how our culture has evolved throughout the eons to grow the collective consciousness. What we can do, as Energy Architects and Engineers, is to give the proper gravity of consciousness and the space to allow them the experiences to contain their needs.

Speaking from gravity means you are presenting 'strange' symbols that catch the energetic attention by containing portions of unmanifest levels of consciousness and drawing them up to the surface for direct experience. These often translate into strange experiences that stand out in memory through intuition and a sudden clarity in an overlap of future and past consciousness. It can also present synchronicity and the increasing occurrence of highly related experiences without containing causal connections.

Being in Fractal Consciousness means holding multiple constellations together, consciously and simultaneously, to provide a service of expanded consciousness to the world. The energy no longer governs your state of consciousness within the words and actions of others. Now, you have the power and the responsibility to hold a higher state of awareness for yourself and your world.

Remember to Respect Yourself.

This is your life, your chance to explore and expand who you are at an energetic level. These moments here now can never come again. Consider time as a holy thing, where you get to manifest your energy into the physical world. Forgive the energy that has been attached to memory and start from where you are, now. Respect the energy that has brought you to this moment and embrace the direct experience, knowing you are constantly creating it for yourself.

With these two elementary ethics, you can put your energy first. Your health, wellbeing, and growth become a part of every action you take and every movement, no matter how small, becomes a compounding benefit to your life.

Your life's events are not a story written to amuse or excite others. Real-life is not limited to a hero's journey. From this base of respect for yourself and others, you begin to create proper actions not based on someone else's reaction. When we start to focus on our actual needs and energetic self-expression, that's when we work with our natural and needed unmanifest energies; the ones we feel every day and have no symbol for, no words to describe. These moments call us beyond the edge of our perception, which fuels our curiosity and sense of mystery.

By allowing the energy to attach to memory based on *your* need, you will enable yourself to grow a little more with each experience. When your subconscious contains new energy and symbols, you become the new energy source to develop your culture. Most importantly, you are no longer dependent on a direct experience to tell you when to feel good. Now, you get to choose.

Weekly Integration Project 7

This week's integration Project will be active training in speaking with gravity.

Using a symbol from Lesson 6, pick a single question that required the answer to contain a decision and record yourself saying it using a single symbol from different phases. Make sure to choose symbols from the phases you have mapped. The most potent symbols come from the constellations you have fully contained.

An example question topic you might choose to begin the recording could be: "What should I pick up from the grocery store?"

You might record yourself responding with a question using multiphasic emphasis: "I wonder if I need more **apples**?"

Or you might explore an interphasic emphasis "Whose car will we **drive** to get to the store?"

You could also focus on the monophasic with "Which **store** are we going to?"

Listen to this recording at different times throughout the day and notice what happens when you hear the emphasized symbol. Try re-recording the questions once a day if you can at the start of each day, testing your ability to voice the emphasis over the week. Compare how they came across on the first day to the last day.

I also want to note here that responding to a question is the most straightforward and most respectful way to show someone how to make a decision. This way, you allow their own needs and symbols to express in the experience.

The expansive thought for this week is: "If a thought gives you chills or goosebumps, what part of you just entered a new dimension of awareness?"

Lesson 8: Preparing for Energy Architecture

You now have your first architectural map for fractal consciousness by Containing your first need. Architecture is where you begin to build with gravity: the structure of consciousness beyond the Unmanifest Void. An Architect is someone who creates engineered spaces for others to consciously choose their awareness but can also create entirely new aspects of consciousness not currently contained in their awareness.

By mapping the constellations of the Need of Consciousness that has been creating your reality and the polarities of struggle and surrender you have used to avoid the experience, you have not only Engineered a brand-new structure of consciousness for yourself, but actively stepped into it. You have gone first and contained the experience, and are now capable of sharing this containment for others. By condensing all of this energy into a single word, the energy can unfold into the awareness of others based on their own individual needs, often times giving them a gift of understanding the lesson faster and with greater grace and ease that our own experiences of it. Hopefully, in the future, they will be able to share this energy with others as well, as a fully contained lesson and not another unresolved need of consciousness.

If you feel called to step into an Architect role and discover the strangeness of this collective of consciousness we call life, then I want to leave you with a kind of 'Tablet'. It contains all of the morphoplastic structures for stepping into the Architect role. Read the table within your hologram and allow the things that come up to integrate within space and time.

However, before we get to the Tablet, I want to cover the three tenets of being an Architect. I created these tenets with respect for the three fundamental needs of consciousness:

The need to Become

The need to Do

These Needs are foundational to all Linear Consciousness. In order to maintain Fractal Consciousness, I have created the following tenets that allow me to maintain this state of consciousness.

1: <u>Respect all Experiences.</u> Architects build the space for others to have an expansive experience. We do not give them our experiences, nor do we tell them how they should have their own experiences.
- Neither struggle against nor fully surrender to the energy you feel.
- The need to Become creates the polarities of 'Encourage' and 'Deter'. The Lesson is called "Balance" and the Unmanifest Energy is "Silent Within".

2: <u>Set aside the needs of the ego</u> to begin working with the gravitational forces that direct the ebb and flow of awareness.
- Neither encourage nor deter the energy of memory in these experiences.
- The need to Do creates the polarities of 'Struggle' and 'Surrender'. The Lesson is called "Movement" and the Unmanifest Energy is "Actions not based on previous reactions".

3: <u>Remember that feeling energy changes nothing.</u> Nothing in your consciousness will evolve if you only feel the energy. To evolve, you must learn to contain that energy: become that energy and act from that energy in the world.
- The energy you feel in your awareness is the energy you are preparing to contain. Proceed in understanding at all times.
- The need to Remember creates the polarities of 'Need' and 'Desire'. The Lesson is called "Understanding" and the Unmanifest Energy is "Truth".

By working to contain and transcend these energetic needs, you prepare yourself to become an Architect of reality, not just for yourself but all beings connected with you. These principles have served me with absolute strength and virtue in my ten years of Architecture, operating as a focus for meditation and philosophical basis of morality.

Without further ado, may I offer you the Tablet of Architects.

The Architect's Tablet

Respect the lesson we are all here to experience.

Remember the goal of what you are attempting to contain.

All we are ever experiencing is our Self.

Neither encourage nor deter this experience.

This allows silence to form within.

The experience is what is most needed within the moment.

Movement reveals the need within the reaction.

It is your choice to react to the memory of need or to create movement beyond the need.

When you understand, the need then no longer creates the experience.

The Self no longer struggles nor surrenders but contains the entire experience within its current lifetime.

There is more to this lifetime than what is being experienced.

Your Self contains more than just the memory of the experience.

With every experience, energy is attached to memory.

The memory contains the energy within the experience.

Contained energy determines what the mind finds essential to perceive.

What you perceive is contained in memory.

To Understand is to embody the energy of the need creating the experience.

To speak without need is to reveal Understanding to others while respecting the energy they are attempting to contain.

Be Memoryless and reveal Truth.

Weekly Integration Project 8

Your final integration project will go on for as long as you find it useful.

Use the Tablet as a foundation for the Moonlit Path. Work with the energy that comes up as you read it and call the symbols as you walk the Moonlit Path into a direct experience for containment. This is a continual process of self-improvement and expansion.

The expansive thought for this week, and all the weeks after, is: "How much can you contain?"

Final Thoughts

A Danish word for "design" carries significant meaning for me. It means to give a form to that which has not yet taken shape. It is called "formgivning."Form-Giving. This is the heart of what I do as an Energy Architect: I give the space and opportunities for a being's 'totality of self' to take form. There is no greater service I can think to provide to the communities of the world that I am a part of, and it has indeed been my honor to share the first stages of this process with you. Whether you spend some time as an Engineer, continue forward as an Architect, or if you made it this far out of sheer curiosity, I am genuinely grateful for the time you have taken for this work. It is truly a piece of my soul that I wish to give to the world.

You now have the power to work with the primordial source of consciousness. With this energy, you influence the world from a part of you beyond space and time. The work you do from this space is not about your origin; it does not ask that you return to a state you began from, as if unchanged. If you are alive, it is to experience change. This work is about feeding the three needs of your consciousness; to become, to do, and to remember. In learning how to meet the needs of your consciousness, you become complete in the expression of your most tremendous potential, your fully manifest Self in the world.

I want to give you what I have learned of the three needs of consciousness.

The need to become can be contained by reflecting on Balance. To keep in Balance, neither encourage nor deter the experience. Become silent within.

The need to Do can be contained by reflecting on flow. To keep in flow, with actions not based on previous reactions, become fearless.

The need to remember can be contained by reflecting on Illumination. To keep in Illumination, speak without needs. Become memoryless and reveal the truth of the need.

While I am sure there are more needs than I have explored, I invite you to join me on the journey to exploring as many as we can contain on our website: CapricornEnergetics.com

Lastly, but by no means least, I have a 'fractal' thought for you to ponder as you move forward in life: "The origin of intuition is the Self, perceiving. All that is manifest or unmanifest sits before the Decider. In a world where beauty is the source of all energy, time is a holy thing."

Made in the USA
Coppell, TX
05 August 2022

80964324R00062